Easy To Make And Use
SCIENCE BULLETIN BOARDS

With Activities To Supplement Your Daily Science Program

by
Imogene Forte
and
Mary Ann Pangle

Incentive Publications, Inc.
Nashville, Tennessee

Edited by Jennifer Goodman
Illustrated by Becky Cutler
Cover by Susan Eaddy

ISBN 0-86530-131-X

Table Of Contents

About This Book

Can science be fun and exciting? Sure! Using bulletin boards to visually reinforce your primary science curriculum will make science a subject all your children will want to learn more about. Providing children with a strong foundation in science is becoming more and more important.

Can bulletin boards be easy to make and still be good? Absolutely! This book provides all the basic artwork needed to create over 56 attractive science bulletin boards. The illustrations may be easily enlarged by using an opaque or overhead projector. Children can also help and learn at the same time by cutting and coloring the illustrations.

Can I plan lessons around my bulletin boards? Yes, and topnotch ones, too! In addition to the artwork, each bulletin board comes complete with skill areas and an activity which has been specifically designed for use with the bulletin board. These skills and activities have been developed according to curriculum content found in current textbooks and state competency requirements so that the bulletin boards can be used along with the regular science textbook.

Can I find the bulletin board I want easily? Yes! If you are interested in a particular content area, just use the table of contents at the beginning of the book. Or, if you are interested in developing a particular skill, the skills index at the back of the book provides an at-a-glance picture of where each skill is presented.

This is your complete science bulletin board resource!

CONTENT EMPHASIS: Plants

SKILLS
Reading/Study: interpreting pictures, reading to find answers to questions
Process Skills: observing, sorting and grouping objects, predicting, questioning, drawing conclusions
Interpersonal Relations & Attitudes: communicating orally and in writing, relating scientific information to everyday experiences, developing an understanding of the relationships among science, technology and society

CONSTRUCTION
1. Enlarge the bulletin board example.
2. Provide resource books.

USE
1. Discuss the importance of plants and their use.
2. Ask students to research the use of plants and write a report.
3. Display the reports near the bulletin board.

CONTENT EMPHASIS: Plants

SKILLS
Reading/Study: interpreting pictures
Process Skills: observing, drawing conclusions
Interpersonal Relations & Attitudes: listening, appreciating the beauty of nature, demonstrating group work skills

CONSTRUCTION
1. Enlarge the bulletin board example.

USE
1. Explain the parts of a plant.
2. Ask different students to bring plants from home.
3. Let students work in small groups and try to identify the plant parts.

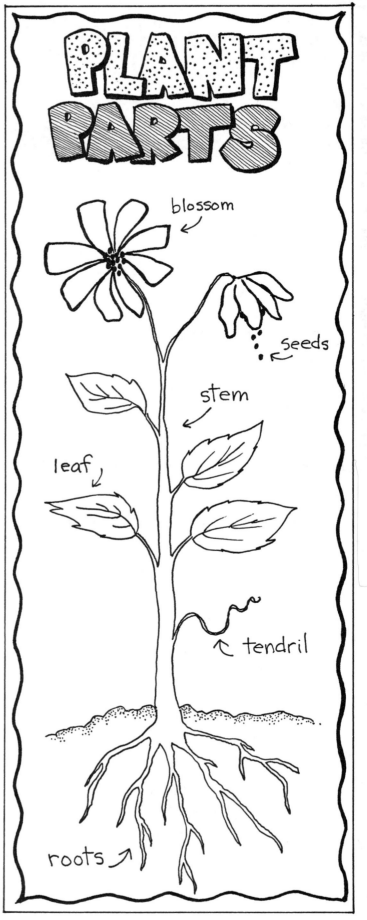

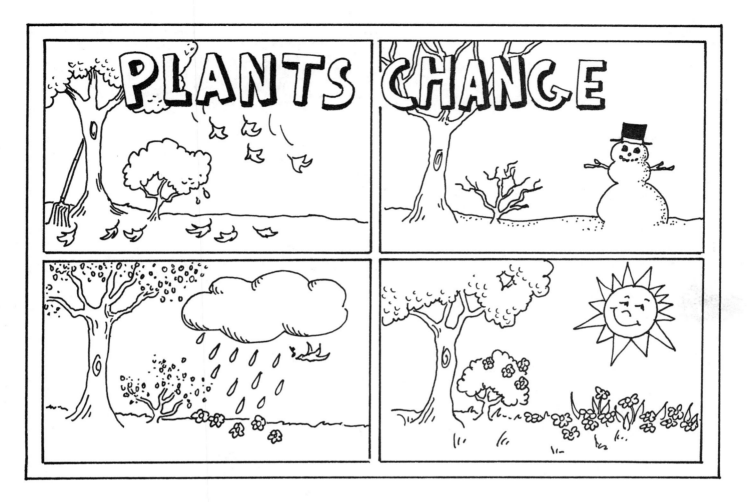

CONTENT EMPHASIS: Plants

SKILLS
Reading/Study: following directions, interpreting pictures
Process Skills: observing, describing, sorting and grouping objects, predicting, questioning, sequencing, drawing conclusions
Interpersonal Relations & Attitudes: cooperating, listening, communicating in pictures, appreciating science for enjoyment, demonstrating group work skills

CONSTRUCTION
1. Divide a large piece of white paper into four spaces.
2. Use a felt tip pen to print the seasons on the paper.
3. Provide resource books and art supplies.

USE
1. Discuss how the seasons affect plants.
2. Let students look at the resource books to see examples of plants in different seasons.
3. Divide the class into four groups. Assign each group a season.
4. Place the paper on the floor and let students draw seasonal scenes illustrating the plants.

CONTENT EMPHASIS: Plants

SKILLS
Reading/Study: interpreting pictures, comparing and contrasting ideas and information
Process Skills: observing, describing, questioning, drawing conclusions
Interpersonal Relations & Attitudes: relating scientific information to everyday experiences

CONSTRUCTION
1. Enlarge the bulletin board example.
2. Provide samples of seeds.
3. Provide small milk containers and soil for students to use to plant seeds.

USE
1. Discuss the different ways in which seeds are spread.
2. Explain what is needed for seeds to grow.
3. Let students plant seeds in milk containers. Place the seed containers near the bulletin board.

CONTENT EMPHASIS: Animals

SKILLS
Reading/Study: comparing and contrasting ideas and information, reading to find answers to questions
Process Skills: describing, predicting, questioning, drawing conclusions
Interpersonal Relations & Attitudes: communicating orally and in writing

CONSTRUCTION
1. Enlarge the bulletin board example.
2. Provide resource books.

USE
1. Discuss animal behavior.
2. Ask students to use the resource books and list animal actions and behaviors which are common to each animal.

ANIMAL ACTIONS

REFLEX

INSTINCT

MIGRATE

HIBERNATION

SOCIAL

LEARNED

CONTENT EMPHASIS: Animals

SKILLS
Reading/Study: following directions
Process Skills: describing, predicting, questioning, drawing conclusions
Interpersonal Relations & Attitudes: communicating orally, appreciating the beauty of nature, appreciating science for enjoyment

CONSTRUCTION
1. Enlarge the bulletin board example.
2. Provide measuring sticks for markers.

USE
1. Discuss the different habitats for animals.
2. Divide the students into two teams.
3. The teacher points to the first space and asks a student from team one to name an animal who lives in the desert. If the student gives a correct answer, the team receives one point, etc. The game continues until one team reaches "finish." The team with the most points wins the game.

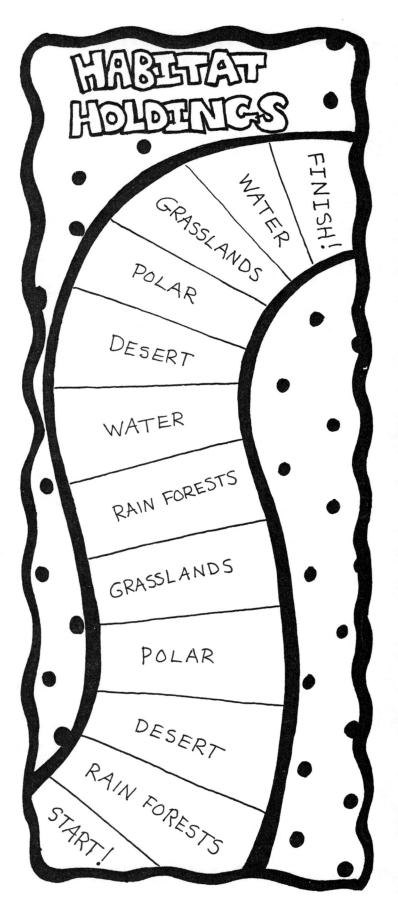

CONTENT EMPHASIS: Animals

SKILLS
Reading/Study: following directions, interpreting pictures, reading to find answers to questions
Process Skills: describing, sorting and grouping, predicting, questioning, drawing conclusions
Interpersonal Relations & Attitudes: communicating orally and in writing, appreciating the beauty of nature, developing decision-making skills

CONSTRUCTION
1. Enlarge the bulletin board example.
2. Prepare an activity sheet asking the students to list the characteristics of each animal. (How they breathe, body covering, how they are born and habitat.)
3. Provide resource books.

USE
1. Discuss animals with backbones.
2. Ask students to complete the vertebrate activity.

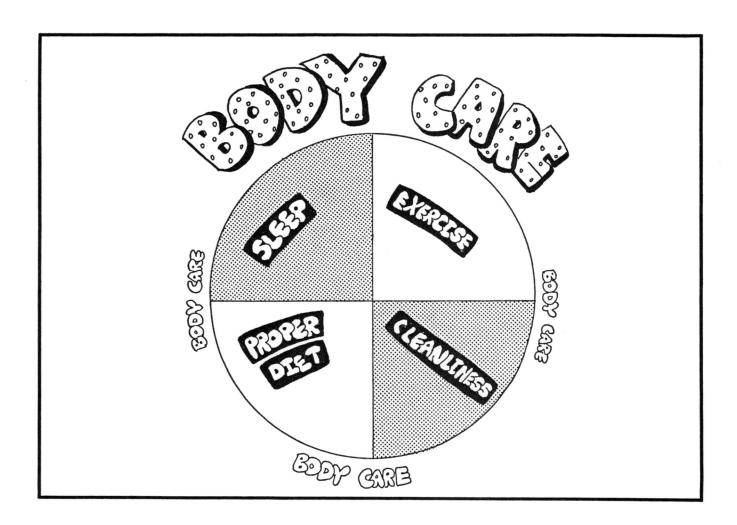

CONTENT EMPHASIS: Human Body

SKILLS
Reading/Study: following directions, interpreting pictures
Process Skills: describing, sorting and grouping objects, predicting, questioning, drawing conclusions
Interpersonal Relations & Attitudes: cooperating, communicating in pictures, appreciating science for enjoyment, relating scientific information to everyday experiences

CONSTRUCTION
1. Cut a large circle from white paper.
2. Print the bulletin board titles on the large circle.
3. Provide art supplies.

USE
1. Discuss body care.
2. Place the large circle on the floor.
3. Divide the students into four groups.
4. Ask each group to illustrate good examples of body care on the large circle of paper.
5. Display the completed Body Care circle on the bulletin board.

CONTENT EMPHASIS: Human Body

SKILLS
Reading/Study: following directions
Process Skills: describing, sorting and grouping objects, predicting, questioning, sequencing, drawing conclusions
Interpersonal Relations & Attitudes: cooperating, communicating orally, appreciating science for enjoyment, relating scientific information to everyday experiences

CONSTRUCTION
1. Enlarge the bulletin board example.

USE
1. Discuss the following systems: respiratory, digestive, circulatory, and excretory.
2. Divide the class into teams with the teacher being the leader.
3. The leader asks one team member to name a part of the respiratory system. If the team member gives the correct answer, the team moves up one rung on the ladder, etc.
4. The game continues in this manner until all team members have a turn. The team who has climbed the ladder the most times wins the game.

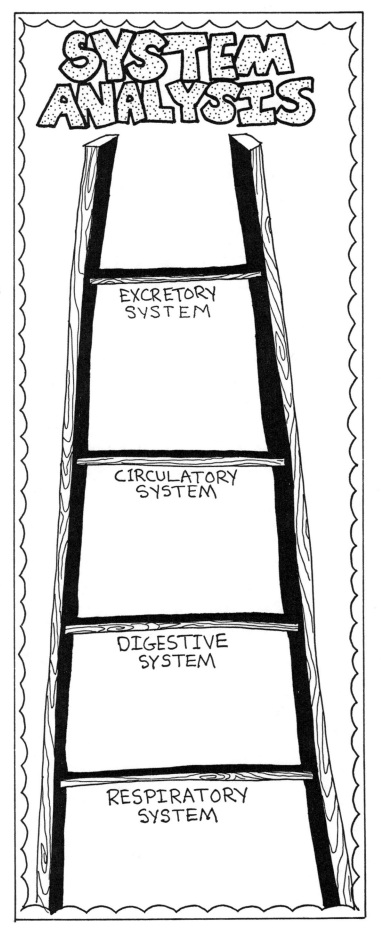

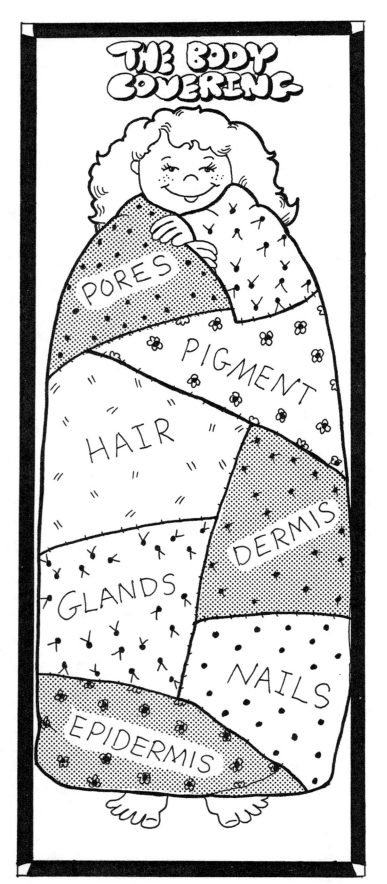

CONTENT EMPHASIS: Human Body

SKILLS
Reading/Study: reading to find answers, following directions
Process Skills: observing, describing, questioning, drawing conclusions
Interpersonal Relations & Attitudes: relating scientific information to everyday experiences, appreciating the history of science

CONSTRUCTION

1. Enlarge the bulletin board example.
2. Enlarge and reproduce one copy of the "Body Covering" activity sheet (shown below) for each student.
3. Provide resource books.

USE

1. Discuss the body covering—skin.
2. Give each student a "Body Covering" activity sheet. Ask each student to write the definition and the function of each part of the skin.

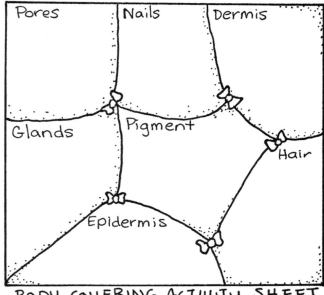

BODY COVERING ACTIVITY SHEET

CONTENT EMPHASIS: Growth and Development

SKILLS
Reading/Study: interpreting pictures, comparing and contrasting ideas and information
Process Skills: observing, describing, predicting, sequencing, drawing conclusions
Interpersonal Relations & Attitudes: listening, communicating orally, appreciating science for enjoyment, relating scientific information to everyday experiences

CONSTRUCTION

1. Enlarge the bulletin board example.

USE

1. Discuss the changes in physical appearance as people grow up.
2. Ask students to bring baby pictures to compare growth.
3. Ask students to list ways in which movement skills have changed.

CONTENT EMPHASIS: Growth and Development

SKILLS
Reading/Study: following directions, comparing and contrasting ideas
Process Skills: describing, questioning, drawing conclusions, identifying problems and possible solutions
Interpersonal Relations & Attitudes: communicating with pictures, appreciating science for enjoyment, developing a sense of responsibility, relating scientific information to everyday experiences

CONSTRUCTION
1.   Use colored construction paper and cut out letters for the bulletin board title. Attach the letters to the bulletin board.
2.   Provide art supplies.

USE
1.   Discuss the ways to stay healthy — correct amount of sleep, nutritious food, plenty of exercise and good hygiene. Emphasize that these rules are essential for growth and development.
2.   Ask students to make posters illustrating ways to stay healthy.
3.   Display the posters on the bulletin board.

CONTENT EMPHASIS: Growth and Development

SKILLS

Reading/Study: following directions, comparing and contrasting ideas and information

Process Skills: observing, measuring, formulating models

Interpersonal Relations & Attitudes: communicating with pictures, appreciating science for enjoyment, relating scientific information to everyday experiences

CONSTRUCTION

1. Enlarge the bulletin board example.
2. Attach it to a door or the wall.
3. Use colored construction paper and cut out letters for the bulletin board title. Attach the letters to the bulletin board.
4. Provide art supplies.

USE

1. Discuss the uniqueness of all individuals. Each person develops differently. Emphasize how each person is special!
2. Ask students to draw pictures of themselves.
3. Display the pictures on the mirror-shaped bulletin board.

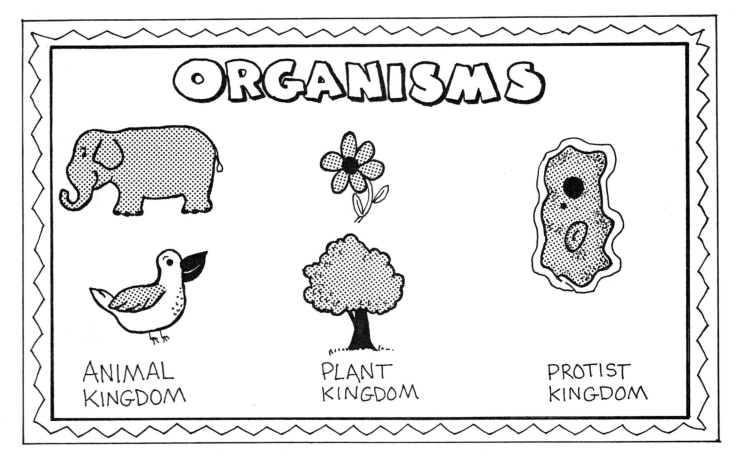

CONTENT EMPHASIS: Microorganisms

SKILLS
Reading/Study: interpreting pictures, judging the relevance of information, locating needed information in the library
Process Skills: observing, questioning, drawing conclusions
Interpersonal Relations & Attitudes: relating scientific information to everyday experiences, appreciating the history of science, developing an understanding of the relationships among science and society

CONSTRUCTION
1. Enlarge the bulletin board example.
2. Provide resource books.

USE
1. Use the bulletin board as an introduction to a unit on microorganisms.
2. Discuss the different characteristics of organisms in each of the three kingdoms.
3. Ask students to read and find out more about each organism kingdom.
4. Provide time for students to share information by giving oral reports.

CONTENT EMPHASIS: Microorganisms

SKILLS
Reading/Study: following directions, constructing diagrams, distinguishing between scientific fact and opinion
Process Skills: observing, questioning, drawing conclusions, collecting data, analyzing data
Interpersonal Relations & Attitudes: cooperating, communicating in pictures, appreciating science for enjoyment, appreciating the beauty of nature, relating scientific information to everyday experiences

CONSTRUCTION
1. Create a tree trunk using brown paper.
2. Provide art supplies.

USE
1. Have a class discussion on different fungi.
2. Take the class on a walking field trip to examine fungi or ask students to bring examples of fungi to school.
3. Ask students to illustrate and cut out one type of fungi that is seen on the field trip.
4. Attach the fungi to the tree on the bulletin board.

CONTENT EMPHASIS: Microorganisms

SKILLS
Reading/Study: reading to find answers to questions, comparing information, distinguishing between fact and opinion
Process Skills: predicting, drawing conclusions, recording data, formulating models
Interpersonal Relations & Attitudes: communicating in pictures, appreciating science for enjoyment, relating scientific information to everyday experiences

CONSTRUCTION
1. Use gift wrap paper and cut out letters for the bulletin board title. Attach the letters to the bulletin board.
2. Provide art supplies.
3. Provide resource books.

USE
1. Discuss how microorganisms can be important to people.
2. Ask students to illustrate how microbes are helpful to people.
3. Display the pictures on the bulletin board.

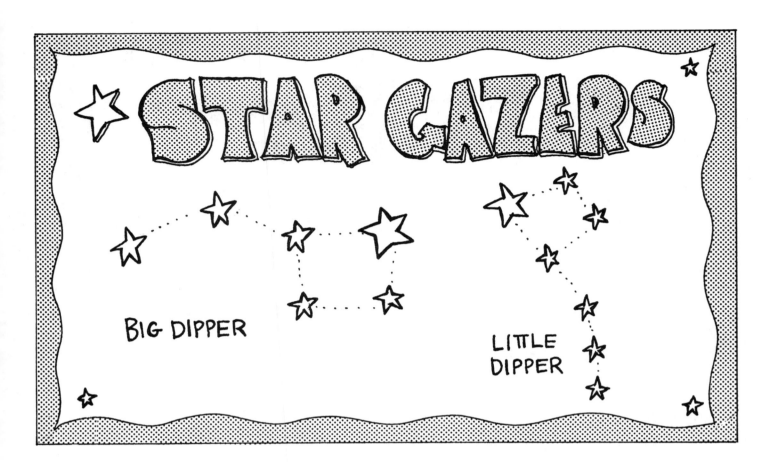

CONTENT EMPHASIS: Astronomy

SKILLS
Reading/Study: following directions, interpreting pictures, locating needed information in the library
Process Skills: observing, describing, sorting and grouping objects, measuring, drawing conclusions, using space/time relations
Interpersonal Relations & Attitudes: cooperating, appreciating science for enjoyment, appreciating the ideas of others, appreciating the beauty of nature, appreciating the history of science

CONSTRUCTION
1. Provide resource books and art supplies.

USE
1. Discuss constellations.
2. Divide the students into small groups.
3. Assign each group a constellation. Ask each group to research the constellation, cut out stars and arrange them to form the constellation.
4. Display the constellations on the bulletin board.

CONTENT EMPHASIS: Astronomy

SKILLS
Reading/Study: following directions, interpreting pictures and symbols, reading for details, writing scientific reports, taking notes
Process Skills: describing, sequencing, drawing conclusions, collecting, recording and analyzing data, measuring
Interpersonal Relations & Attitudes: cooperating, communicating orally and in writing, appreciating science for enjoyment, appreciating the history of science, demonstrating group work skills

CONSTRUCTION
1. Create a sun shape using orange construction paper.
2. Cut letters for the names of the planets.
3. Provide resource books and art supplies.

USE
1. Discuss the solar system.
2. Divide the students into nine groups.
3. Assign each group a planet. Ask each group to make the planet shape and attach it to the bulletin board.
4. Ask each group to create a model of their assigned planet using papier mâché.
5. Ask the students in each group to write a report on their assigned planet.

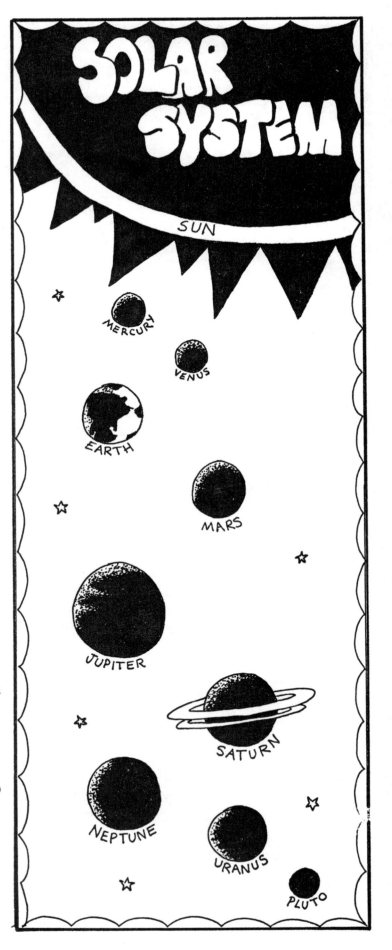

CONTENT EMPHASIS: Meteorology

SKILLS
Reading/Study: following directions
Process Skills: describing, drawing conclusions
Interpersonal Relations & Attitudes: cooperating, appreciating science for enjoyment

CONSTRUCTION
1. Enlarge the bulletin board example.
2. Provide a measuring stick for a marker.

USE
1. Review the vocabulary words related to meteorology.
2. Let one student at a time pretend to be the person reporting the weather on television.
3. The student goes to the bulletin board and gives the weather report by pointing to a shape and saying the definition of the vocabulary word.

CONTENT EMPHASIS: Meteorology

SKILLS
Reading/Study: reading to find answers to questions, interpreting pictures, interpreting symbols, writing scientific reports
Process Skills: observing, sorting and grouping objects, predicting, questioning, drawing conclusions
Interpersonal Relations & Attitudes: communicating orally and in writing, relating scientific information to everyday experiences

CONSTRUCTION
1. Enlarge the bulletin board example.
2. Provide resource books.
3. Provide art supplies.

USE
1. Discuss storms.
2. Ask each student to research the various types of storms and write a report on each type.
3. Let students make and decorate booklet covers for the storm reports.
4. Display the booklets near the bulletin board.

CONTENT EMPHASIS: Meteorology

SKILLS
Reading/Study: following directions, reading to find answers, interpreting pictures
Process Skills: observing, questioning, describing, sorting and grouping objects, drawing conclusions, collecting data, recording data
Interpersonal Relations & Attitudes: communicating orally and in writing, appreciating science for enjoyment, appreciating the beauty of nature, relating scientific information to everyday experiences

CONSTRUCTION
1. Enlarge the bulletin board example.
2. Make clouds from different materials — cotton, yarn, plastic, paper.
3. Provide resource books.

USE
1. Discuss clouds and their relationship to weather.
2. Ask students to observe the clouds for one week and record the information.
3. Assign students a homework project using various materials to illustrate the different types of clouds.
4. Display the projects near the bulletin board.

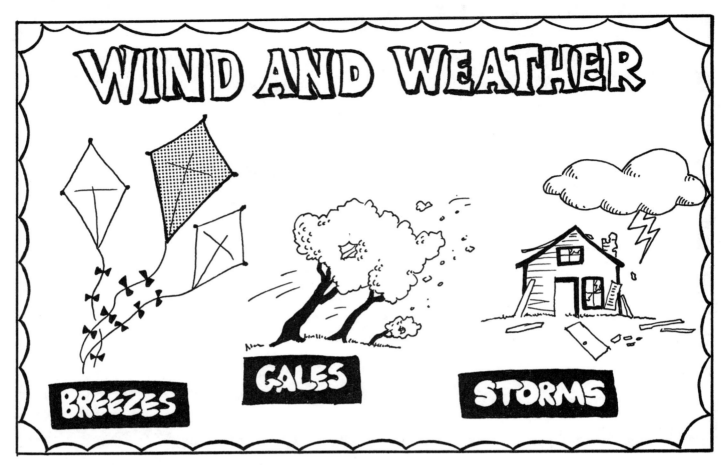

CONTENT EMPHASIS: Meteorology

SKILLS
Reading/Study: following directions, comparing and contrasting ideas and information
Process Skills: observing, describing, predicting, measuring, questioning, drawing conclusions
Interpersonal Relations & Attitudes: communicating in pictures, appreciating science for enjoyment, relating scientific information to everyday experiences

CONSTRUCTION
1. Use colored construction paper and cut out letters for the title of the bulletin board example. Attach the letters to the bulletin board.
2. Print the words, Breezes, Gales and Storms on strips of colored construction paper. Attach them to the bulletin board.
3. Provide art supplies and scissors.

USE
1. Discuss wind and its relationship to the weather.
2. Ask students to draw and cut out pictures illustrating what kinds of things occur when the wind blows (hat blowing off, leaves falling off trees).
3. Display the pictures on the bulletin board.

CONTENT EMPHASIS: Geology

SKILLS
Reading/Study: interpreting pictures, locating needed information in the library
Process Skills: observing, describing, sorting and grouping objects, questioning, drawing conclusions
Interpersonal Relations & Attitudes: listening, appreciating the beauty of nature, communicating orally

CONSTRUCTION
1. Enlarge the bulletin board example.
2. Provide resource books.

USE
1. Discuss how rocks are formed.
2. Ask students to find pictures of the various types of rocks in books.
3. Let students bring in different types of rocks and present a "rock show."

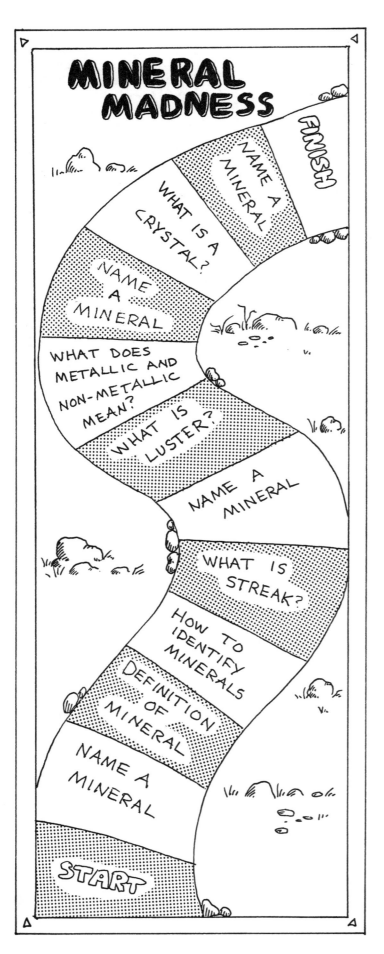

CONTENT EMPHASIS: Geology

SKILLS
Reading/Study: following directions, comparing and contrasting ideas and information
Process Skills: describing, drawing conclusions
Interpersonal Relations & Attitudes: cooperating, communicating orally, appreciating science for enjoyment, demonstrating group work skills

CONSTRUCTION
1. Enlarge the bulletin board example.
2. Provide measuring sticks for markers.
3. Provide a die.

USE
1. Discuss minerals.
2. Let two students at a time play "Mineral Madness."
3. The first player throws the die and moves the correct number of spaces. The player must give an answer to what is written in the space. If the answer is correct, the player moves forward one space. If an incorrect answer is given, the player loses a turn.
4. The game continues until one player reaches "finish" to win the game.

CONTENT EMPHASIS: Geology

SKILLS
Reading/Study: interpreting pictures, reading to find answers to questions
Process Skills: describing, predicting, questioning, drawing conclusions
Interpersonal Relations & Attitudes: listening, appreciating the history of science

CONSTRUCTION
1. Enlarge the bulletin board example.
2. Provide resource books.
3. Provide art supplies

USE
1. Discuss the layers of the earth.
2. Ask students to read about, list and write a description of each layer of the earth.
3. Ask each student to draw and cut out a circle using manila paper. On each circle, have students illustrate the layers of the earth.
4. Display the pictures on or near the bulletin board.

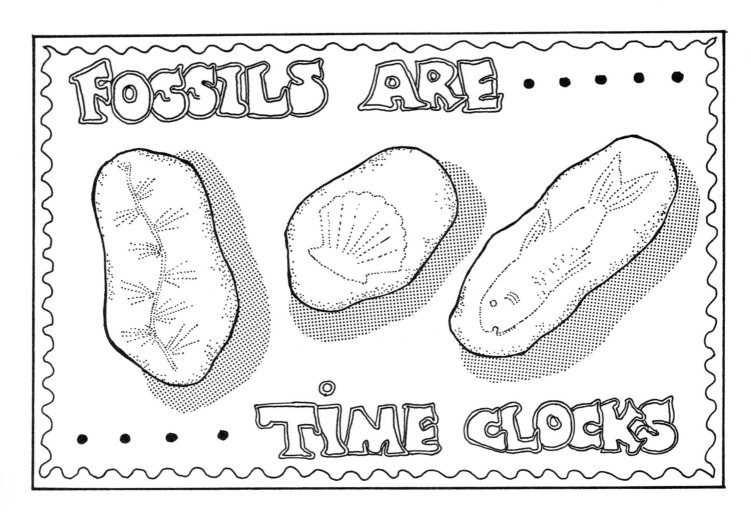

CONTENT EMPHASIS: Geology

SKILLS
Reading/Study: following directions, interpreting pictures
Process Skills: observing, predicting, questioning, drawing conclusions
Interpersonal Relations & Attitudes: listening, cooperating, appreciating science for enjoyment, appreciating the history of science, demonstrating group work skills

CONSTRUCTION
1. Enlarge the bulletin board example.
2. Provide plaster of Paris, water, paper cups and petroleum jelly.

USE
1. Discuss fossils.
2. Ask students to bring a shell, bone or something similar, to case a fossil.
3. Mix plaster of Paris and water together and pour in paper cups. Rub petroleum jelly on the shell. Place the shell on the plaster of Paris mixture and let dry overnight. The next day, put another layer of plaster of Paris in the cup. When dry, remove from cup.
4. Display the fossil casts near the bulletin board.

CONTENT EMPHASIS: Oceanography

SKILLS
Reading/Study Skills: following directions, reading for details, comparing ideas
Process Skills: describing, questioning, drawing conclusions, predicting
Interpersonal Relations & Attitudes: developing an understanding of the relationship among science, technology and society, cooperating

CONSTRUCTION
1. Cover the bulletin board with blue paper.
2. Cut out the shapes using different colored construction paper. Write one of the following words on each shape: food, salt, manganese, diamonds, gold, oil, gas, iodine, pearls. Attach the shapes to the bulletin board.
3. Attach a manila folder to the bulletin board.

USE
1. Lead a class discussion on ocean resources.
2. Divide the class into groups and provide resource books.
3. Ask each group to write two riddles for each ocean resource given.
4. Place the riddles in the manila folder.
5. Allow students to go to the bulletin board individually or in small groups to solve the riddles.

CONTENT EMPHASIS: Oceanography

SKILLS
Reading/Study: interpreting pictures
Process Skills: analyzing data, drawing conclusions
Interpersonal Relations & Attitudes: relating scientific information to everyday experiences

CONSTRUCTION
1. Use brown construction paper to illustrate soil, a shade of blue construction paper to illustrate a river and another shade of blue construction paper to illustrate the ocean on the bottom of the bulletin board.
2. Cut strips of black construction paper for arrows.
3. Use cotton to make a cloud.
4. Use gray construction paper to make raindrops.
5. Use white paper to make snowflakes.

USE
1. The bulletin board is used as a teaching tool to explain the water cycle and the importance of the ocean in the process.

CONTENT EMPHASIS: Oceanography

SKILLS
Reading/Study: interpreting tables, graphs and diagrams
Process Skills: observing, using space relations
Interpersonal Relations & Attitudes: relating scientific information to everyday experiences

CONSTRUCTION
1. Attach a world map to the bulletin board.
2. Print ocean route questions on a piece of paper and reproduce a sheet for each student. The level of difficulty can be varied for different grades. Example: What ocean route would be used to travel from Japan to New York?
3. Attach a manila folder to the bulletin board and place the ocean route activities in the folder.

USE
1. Discuss the location of each ocean in relation to the countries of the world.
2. Ask students to use the map to find the ocean routes which would be used to travel between countries.

CONTENT EMPHASIS: Energy and the Environment

SKILLS
Reading/Study: reading to find answers, taking notes, writing reports
Process Skills: describing, collecting and analyzing data
Interpersonal Relations & Attitudes: communicating in writing, relating scientific information to everyday experiences

CONSTRUCTION
1.   Enlarge the example of the bulletin board.
2.   Provide resource books.
3.   Provide art supplies.

USE
1.   Have a class discussion on the various types of energy.
2.   Divide the class into seven groups. Ask each group to research a type of energy, write a short report, prepare illustrations of the energy type and present the project to the class.
3.   Display the energy illustrations on the bulletin board.

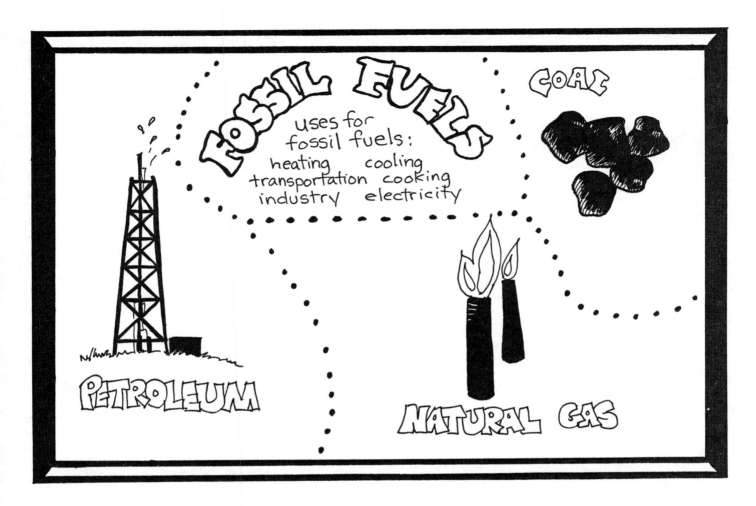

CONTENT EMPHASIS: Energy and the Environment

SKILLS
Reading/Study: reading to find answers, locating needed information in the library, writing scientific reports
Process Skills: predicting, questioning, drawing conclusions, identifying problems and possible solutions
Interpersonal Relations & Attitudes: communicating in writing, understanding how our activities affect our environment, developing an understanding of the relationship between science and society

CONSTRUCTION
1. Enlarge the example of the bulletin board.
2. Provide resource books.

USE
1. Have a class discussion on fossil fuels.
2. Ask students to write a report titled, "Fossil Fuels and Our Environment."
3. After students have shared the reports, display them near the bulletin board.

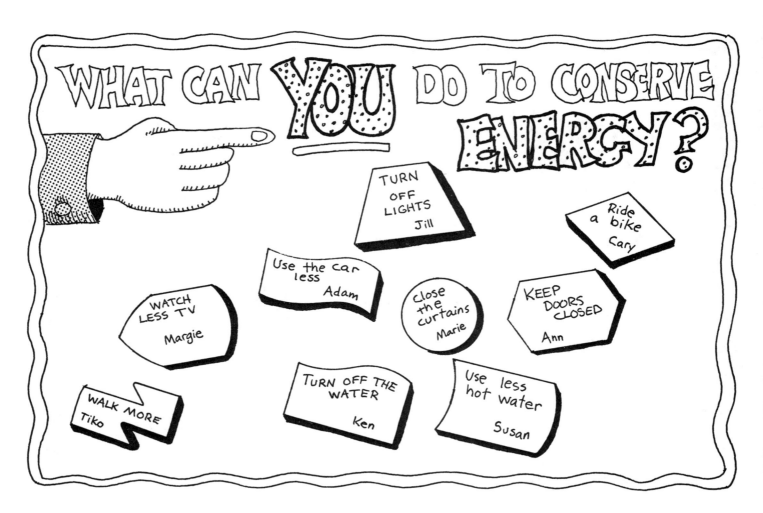

CONTENT EMPHASIS: Energy and the Environment

SKILLS
Reading/Study: comparing and contrasting ideas and information
Process Skills: predicting, questioning, drawing conclusions, identifying problems and possible solutions
Interpersonal Relations & Attitudes: communicating orally and in writing, understanding how our activities affect the environment, appreciating the beauty of nature, developing a sense of responsibility

CONSTRUCTION
1.   Enlarge the hand on the bulletin board example.
2.   Use colored construction paper and cut out letters for the bulletin board title. Attach the letters to the bulletin board.
3.   Provide colored construction paper, felt tip pens and scissors.

USE
1.   Discuss ways to conserve energy.
2.   Ask students to make a list of ways he or she can conserve energy.
3.   Ask students to create an interesting shape with a piece of colored construction paper. Use a felt tip pen to write one way to conserve energy.
4.   Display the conservation ideas on the bulletin board.

CONTENT EMPHASIS: Man's Effect on the Earth

SKILLS

Reading/Study: following directions, judging the relevance of information

Process Skills: describing, predicting, drawing conclusions, identifying problems and possible solutions

Interpersonal Relations & Attitudes: communicating orally, appreciating science for enjoyment, understanding how our activities affect our environment, developing a sense of responsibility, developing decision making skills

CONSTRUCTION

1. Use sheets of colored construction paper to create a train shape and letters for the bulletin board title. Attach them to the bulletin board.
2. On strips of poster board, print the following words: pollution, smog, environment, sanitary landfill, recycle, air pollution, water pollution, land pollution, carbon monoxide, noise pollution, Environmental Protection Agency (EPA), solid waste, liquid waste, pesticides, sulfur dioxide, sewage treatment, etc.
3. Place the word cards in the train cars.

USE

1. Introduce the environmental vocabulary list.
2. To reinforce the environmental vocabulary, play the "Environmental Express" game.
3. Divide the class into two groups.
4. One player from one group draws a word card from the train, pronounces the word/words and gives the definition. If the answer given is correct, the player's team receives one point. The game continues in the same manner until all of the word cards have been used. The team with the most points wins the game.

CONTENT EMPHASIS: Man's Effect on the Earth

SKILLS
Reading/Study: reading to find answers to questions, taking notes
Process Skills: observing, describing, predicting, drawing conclusions, identifying problems and possible solutions
Interpersonal Relations & Attitudes: understanding how our activities affect the environment, developing a sense of responsibility, relating scientific information to everyday experiences

CONSTRUCTION
1. Enlarge the bulletin board example.
2. Provide resource books.

USE
1. Discuss the various efforts being made to clean up the environment.
2. Ask students to list ways their city or town is trying to improve the environment. Provide time for students to share their ideas.

CONTENT EMPHASIS: Man's Effect on the Earth

SKILLS
Reading/Study: reading to find answers to questions, comparing and contrasting ideas and information
Process Skills: observing, predicting, questioning, drawing conclusions
Interpersonal Relations & Attitudes: understanding how our activities affect the environment, developing a sense of responsibility, respecting rules and authority, understanding that science is subject to change

CONSTRUCTION
1. Use red construction paper to create a shape to resemble a school. Attach the school to the bulletin board.
2. Use black construction paper and cut out letters for the bulletin board title. Attach them to the bulletin board.
3. Provide art supplies.

USE
1. Introduce the concept of population density.
2. Give each student a piece of drawing paper. (The size will be in relation to the bulletin board size.) Ask the students to draw and cut out their whole body shape.
3. Arrange the pictures on the bulletin board to show population density.

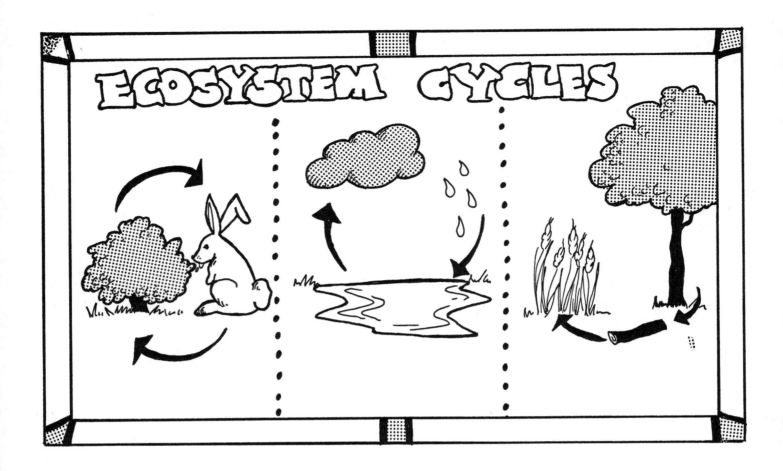

CONTENT EMPHASIS: Ecosystems

SKILLS
Reading/Study: reading to find answers to questions, interpreting pictures, taking notes
Process Skills: observing, predicting, sequencing, analyzing data, drawing conclusions
Interpersonal Relations & Attitudes: understanding how our activities affect the environment, relating scientific information to everyday experiences, appreciating the history of science

CONSTRUCTION
1. Enlarge the bulletin board example.
2. Provide art supplies.

USE
1. Define "ecosystem" to students — the way living and non-living things interact.
2. Discuss ecosystem cycles.
3. Ask students to draw ecosystem cycles. Display the pictures near the bulletin board.

CONTENT EMPHASIS: Ecosystems

SKILLS
Reading/Study: interpreting pictures, constructing diagrams, summarizing
Process Skills: describing, predicting, sequencing, drawing conclusions, formulating models
Interpersonal Relations & Attitudes: communicating in pictures, understanding how our activities affect the environment, relating scientific information to everyday experiences

CONSTRUCTION
1. Enlarge the bulletin board example.
2. Provide art materials.

USE
1. Discuss food chains and their relationship to the ecosystem.
2. Ask students to illustrate food chains.
3. Invite another class to visit the classroom and let students explain the food chains.

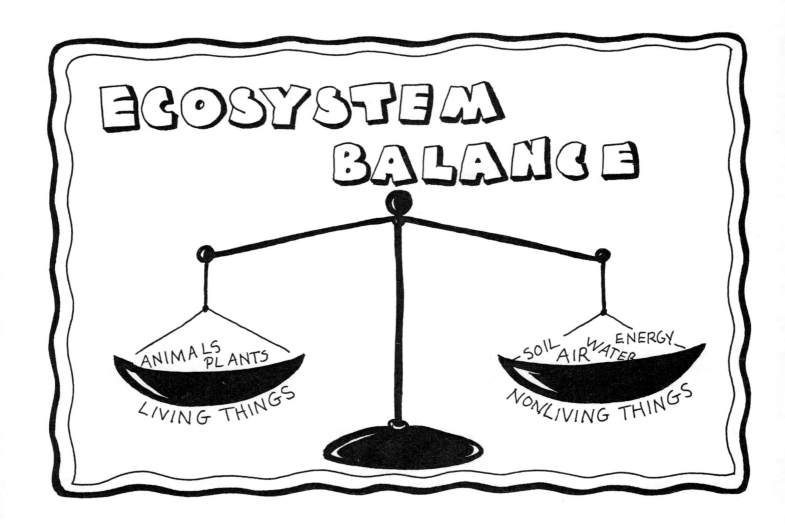

CONTENT EMPHASIS: Ecosystems

SKILLS
Reading/Study: reading to find answers to questions, writing scientific reports, taking notes
Process Skills: describing, predicting, drawing conclusions, collecting data, analyzing data
Interpersonal Relations & Attitudes: communicating in writing, understanding how our activities affect the environment, relating scientific information to everyday experiences

CONSTRUCTION
1. Enlarge the bulletin board example.
2. Provide resource books.

USE
1. Discuss the Earth as an ecosystem and the balance of nature.
2. Ask students to research and write a report on the importance of the balance of nature.

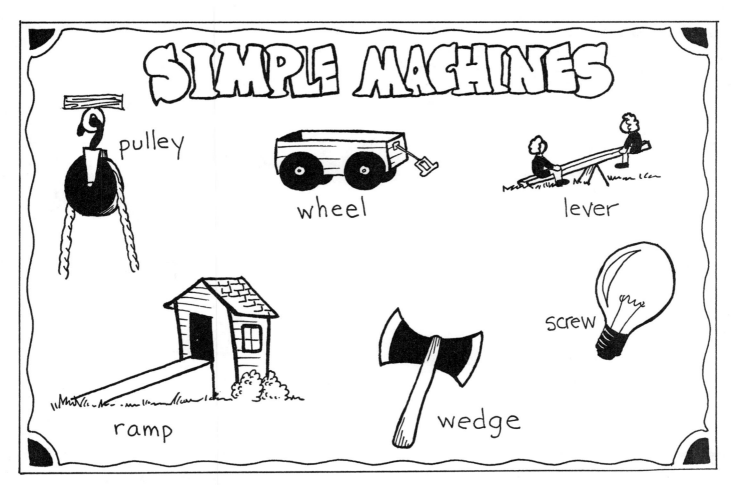

CONTENT EMPHASIS: Machines and Work

SKILLS
Reading/Study: interpreting pictures, comparing and contrasting ideas and information
Process Skills: observing
Interpersonal Relations & Attitudes: appreciating science for enjoyment, relating scientific information to everyday experiences, demonstrating group work skills

CONSTRUCTION
1. Enlarge the pictures on the bulletin board example with an overhead projector. Attach the pictures to the bulletin board.
2. Attach a large piece of brown paper to the wall near the bulletin board. Provide art supplies for students to draw a mural.

USE
1. Discuss simple machines. Use the pictures on the bulletin board to develop and reinforce understanding of simple machines and their uses.
2. Ask students to plan and draw a mural showing people using different kinds of simple machines.
3. Ask each student to write a brief report explaining the purpose and uses of the machine he or she draws. Provide a time for these reports to be read aloud to the entire group.

CONTENT EMPHASIS: Machines and Work

SKILLS
Reading/Study: interpreting pictures
Process Skills: observing
Interpersonal Relations & Attitudes: developing an understanding of the relationships among science, technology and society

CONSTRUCTION
1. Enlarge the pictures on the bulletin board example or cut examples of complex machines from magazines. Attach the pictures to the bulletin board.

USE
1. The bulletin board is used to help students distinguish between simple and complex machines.
2. Ask the students to make a list of complex machines for each category which is listed on the bulletin board.

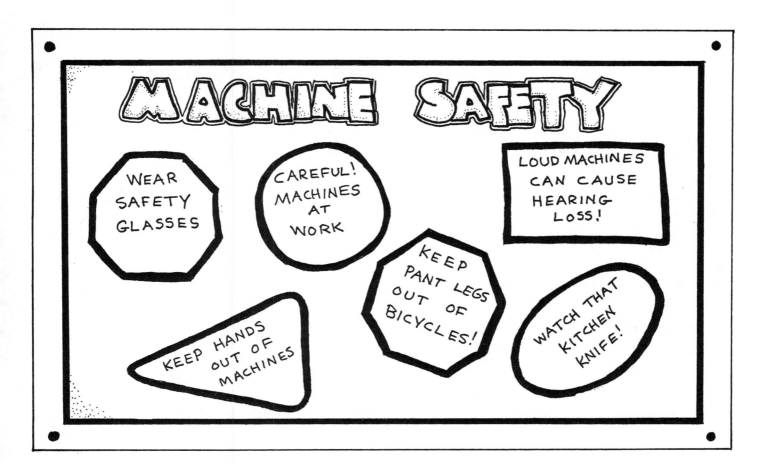

CONTENT EMPHASIS: Machines and Work

SKILLS
Reading/Study: following directions
Process Skills: drawing conclusions, identifying problems and possible solutions
Interpersonal Relations & Attitudes: developing a sense of responsibility

CONSTRUCTION
1. Create a sign and label it, "Careful: Machines At Work."
2. Provide art supplies for students to make signs.

USE
1. Have a class discussion on machine safety.
2. Ask the students to make machine safety signs and write a safety slogan for each sign.
3. Display the signs on the bulletin board and around the classroom.

CONTENT EMPHASIS: Electricity and Magnetism

SKILLS
Reading/Study: interpreting pictures, comparing information
Process Skills: observing, predicting, questioning, drawing conclusions
Interpersonal Relations & Attitudes: appreciating science for enjoyment, relating scientific information to everyday experiences

CONSTRUCTION
1. Cover the back of a bookcase or attach paper to a wall in the classroom.
2. Enlarge the example of the bulletin board.
3. Place a table near the bulletin board and provide magnets and metal objects for students to experiment with.

USE
1. Introduce a teaching unit on Electricity and Magnetism with this bulletin board.
2. Provide time for students to experiment with the magnets and metal objects.

Magnets can be different shapes

The ends of a magnet are called poles

Magnets can attract one another

Magnets can repel one another

CONTENT EMPHASIS: Electricity and Magnetism

SKILLS
Reading/Study: interpreting pictures, comparing information
Process Skills: observing, questioning, drawing conclusions
Interpersonal Relations & Attitudes: appreciating the history of science

CONSTRUCTION
1. Enlarge the example of the bulletin board. This can be a "mini bulletin board."

USE
1. Discuss how the Earth is a magnet.
2. Introduce students to a magnetic compass.
3. If possible, show students a lodestone and relate some information about this rock.

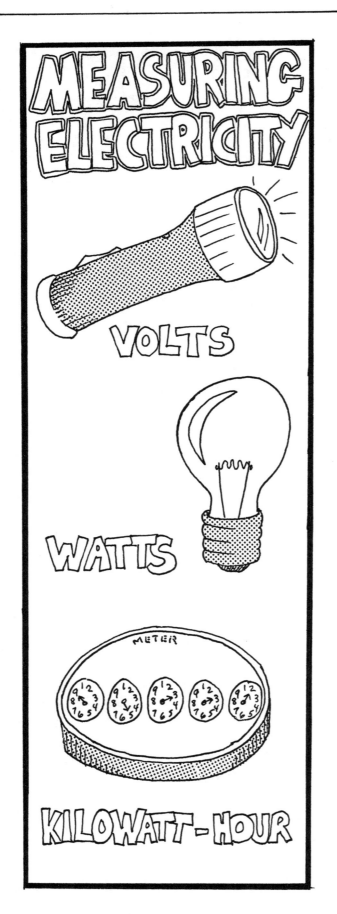

CONTENT EMPHASIS: Electricity and Magnetism

SKILLS
Reading/Study: judging the relevance of information, reading for details, comparing ideas and information
Process Skills: describing, drawing conclusions
Interpersonal Relations & Attitudes: cooperating, appreciating the ideas of others, relating scientific information to everyday experiences, developing an understanding of the relationships among science, technology and society

CONSTRUCTION
1. Enlarge the bulletin board example.
2. Provide art materials for students to make kilowatt-hour meters.

USE
1. Discuss the different ways that electricity can be measured.
2. Ask students to make kilowatt-hour meters from construction paper.
3. Let students exchange kilowatt-hour meters. Ask the students to "read" the meters by writing the numbers on a piece of paper.

CONTENT EMPHASIS: Electricity and Magnetism

SKILLS
Reading/Study: reading to find answers, judging the relevance of information, distinguishing between scientific fact and opinion
Process Skills: predicting, drawing conclusions
Interpersonal Relations & Attitudes: appreciating science for enjoyment

CONSTRUCTION
1. Use scraps of material and cut out letters for the bulletin board title. Attach the letters to the bulletin board.
2. Provide art supplies for students to illustrate examples of static electricity.

USE
1. Complete the bulletin board as a follow-up activity from teaching static electricity.
2. Ask students to illustrate examples of static electricity.
3. Display the pictures on the bulletin board.

CONTENT EMPHASIS: Electricity and Magnetism

SKILLS

Reading/Study: following directions, comparing ideas and information, distinguishing between scientific fact and opinion

Process Skills: sorting, predicting, questioning, drawing conclusions, identifying problems and possible solutions

Interpersonal Relations & Attitudes: communicating in writing, developing a sense of responsibility, respecting rules and authority, developing decision-making skills

CONSTRUCTION

1. Enlarge the bulletin board example.
2. Provide felt tip pens.
3. Prepare an activity sheet for each student to write electricity safety rules on.

USE

1. Have a class discussion concerning the importance of safety and electricity.
2. Ask students to write electricity safety rules on the activity sheet.
3. Provide time for students to share the rules. Let the students decide which of the rules is most important.

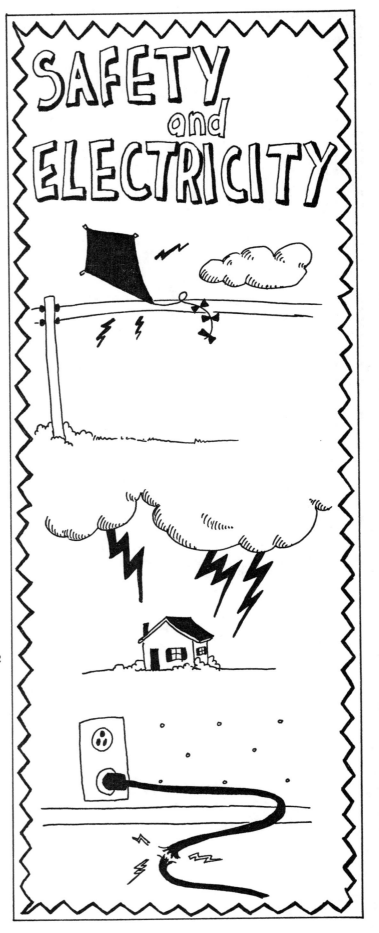

CONTENT EMPHASIS: Sound

SKILLS
Reading/Study: comparing and contrasting ideas and information, reading for details
Process Skills: observing, describing, predicting, questioning, drawing conclusions
Interpersonal Relations & Attitudes: listening, communicating orally, appreciating science for enjoyment, relating scientific information to everyday experiences

CONSTRUCTION
1. Enlarge the bulletin board example.
2. Provide resource books.
3. Provide solid objects and containers of water.

USE
1. Explain that sound travels in waves and through air, solids and water.
2. Ask students to experiment with the solid objects and water to see how sound travels.

CONTENT EMPHASIS: Sound

SKILLS
Reading/Study: following directions, judging the relevance of information
Process Skills: observing, predicting, questioning, drawing conclusions
Interpersonal Relations & Attitudes: listening, communicating orally and in pictures, appreciating science for enjoyment, relating scientific information to everyday experiences

CONSTRUCTION
1. Enlarge the bulletin board example.
2. Provide art supplies.

USE
1. Ask the students to make a list of different sounds.
2. Provide time for students to share their "sound lists."
3. Ask students to draw examples of objects or people that make sounds.
4. Display the "sound pictures" on the bulletin board.

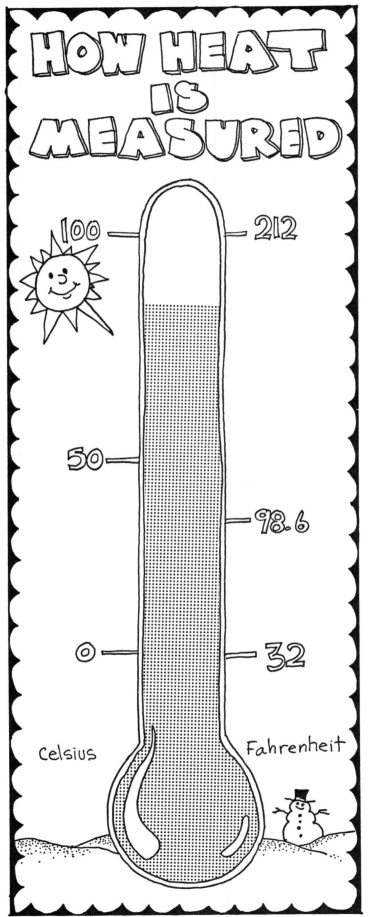

CONTENT EMPHASIS: Heat

SKILLS

Reading/Study: interpreting pictures, comparing and contrasting ideas and information

Process Skills: observing, describing, measuring, questioning, drawing conclusions

Interpersonal Relations & Attitudes: appreciating science for enjoyment, relating scientific information to everyday experiences

CONSTRUCTION

1. Enlarge the bulletin board example.
2. Prepare an activity which requires students to transfer degrees in Fahrenheit to degrees in Celsius. Example: 32°F is _____°C.
3. Provide thermometers.

USE

1. Discuss how heat is measured.
2. Ask students to look at the thermometers and complete the activity.

CONTENT EMPHASIS: Heat

SKILLS
Reading/Study: following directions, interpreting pictures, locating needed information in the library
Process Skills: predicting, questioning, observing, drawing conclusions
Interpersonal Relations & Attitudes: communicating in pictures, appreciating science for enjoyment, relating scientific information to everyday experiences

CONSTRUCTION
1. Use colored construction paper and cut out letters for the bulletin board title. Attach the letters to the bulletin board.
2. Provide art supplies.

USE
1. Discuss how heat can make matter expand and contract.
2. Ask students to illustrate objects in which matter can be expanded or contracted by heat.
3. Display the pictures on the bulletin board.

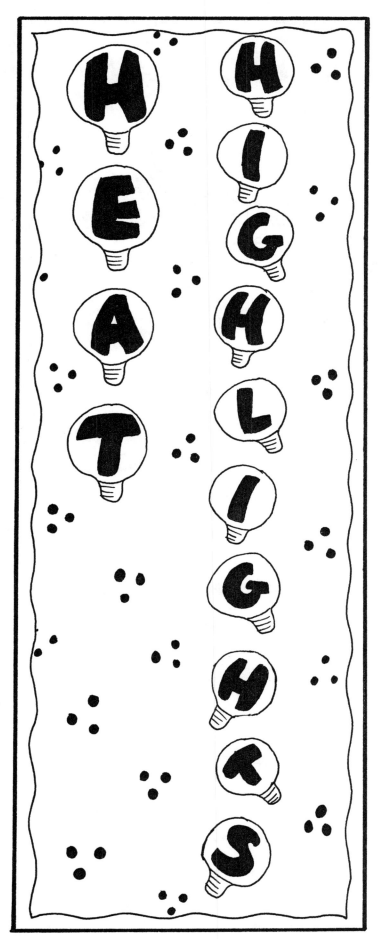

CONTENT EMPHASIS: Heat

SKILLS
Reading/Study: following directions, comparing and contrasting ideas and information
Process Skills: describing, drawing conclusions
Interpersonal Relations & Attitudes: cooperating, communicating orally, appreciating science for enjoyment, respecting rules and authority, relating scientific information to everyday experiences, demonstrating group work skills

CONSTRUCTION
1. Enlarge the bulletin board example.
2. Write one of the following words under each "letter light."

conduct	convection
conductor	radiation
insulate	temperature
insulator	expand
conduction	contract
heat transfer	thermometer
Celsius	Fahrenheit

3. Provide a measuring stick to be used as a pointer.

USE
1. Divide the class into two teams.
2. The teacher points to one "letter light" and turns it over.
3. One player from team one must pronounce the word and say the correct definition to score one point. One player from team two must do the same thing, etc. The game continues until all of the "letter lights" have been used.

CONTENT EMPHASIS: Light

SKILLS
Reading/Study: comparing and contrasting ideas and information, locating needed information in the library
Process Skills: observing, predicting, questioning, drawing conclusions
Interpersonal Relations & Attitudes: relating scientific information to everyday experiences

CONSTRUCTION
1. Enlarge the bulletin board example.
2. Provide different examples of lenses.

USES
1. Discuss light and lenses.
2. Divide the class into groups and let them examine the examples of lenses.

CONTENT EMPHASIS: Light

SKILLS
Reading/Study: following directions, comparing and contrasting ideas and information, locating needed information in the library, summarizing, taking notes
Process Skills: describing, predicting, questioning, drawing conclusions, collecting, recording and analyzing data, formulating models
Interpersonal Relations & Attitudes: communicating orally and in writing, appreciating science for enjoyment, appreciating the history of science

CONSTRUCTION
1. Enlarge the bulletin board example.
2. Provide resource books.

USE
1. Have a class discussion on telescopes and how light is important in their use.
2. Ask each student to research and take notes on the making and use of telescopes.
3. Ask students to write a report titled "Light and the Telescope."
4. Provide a time for the reports to be presented to the group.

CONTENT EMPHASIS: Matter and Energy

SKILLS
Reading/Study: interpreting pictures, comparing and contrasting information
Process Skills: predicting, questioning, drawing conclusions
Interpersonal Relations & Attitudes: relating scientific information to everyday experiences

CONSTRUCTION
1. Divide the bulletin board into four equal parts. Label each part as shown on the bulletin board example.
2. Provide art materials for students to illustrate examples of how matter can change forms.

USE
1. Have a class discussion on how matter can change forms.
2. Ask students to illustrate examples of how matter can change forms.
3. Display the pictures on the bulletin board.

CONTENT EMPHASIS: Matter and Energy

SKILLS
Reading/Study: following directions, judging the relevance of information
Process Skills: sorting, predicting, questioning, drawing conclusions, analyzing data
Interpersonal Relations & Attitudes: appreciating science for enjoyment, understanding how our activities affect the environment, relating scientific information to everyday experiences

CONSTRUCTION
1. Enlarge the example of the bulletin board. Cut slots where dotted lines are on the bulletin board.
2. Write examples of matter that have physical changes and chemical changes on strips of poster board. Example: sawing wood (physical), rusting bicycle (chemical), etc. Place the word cards in a manila folder and attach it to the bulletin board.

USE
1. Have a discussion on physical and chemical changes of matter.
2. Ask students to take the strips of poster board and program them into the computer by placing the strip in the correct slot.

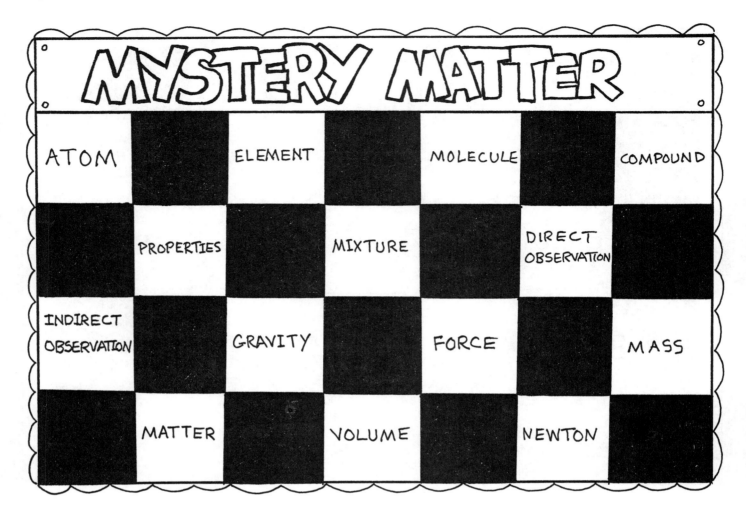

CONTENT EMPHASIS: Matter and Energy

SKILLS
Reading/Study: following directions, reading for details
Process Skills: questioning, drawing conclusions, analyzing data, using a key
Interpersonal Relations & Attitudes: listening, relating scientific information to everyday experiences, developing decision-making skills

CONSTRUCTION
1. Write one matter vocabulary word on a piece of 8" x 10" colored construction paper. Attach the words "face down" to the bulletin board, alternating with a black piece of colored construction paper.
2. Make an answer key by writing the definition for each word on a piece of posterboard.
3. Prepare an activity sheet similar to the bulletin board.

USE
1. Introduce a new "matter" vocabulary word each day by turning over the word on the bulletin board.
2. At the end of 14 days, all of the words will be introduced.
3. Give each student the prepared activity sheet and have them write the definition under each word.

Skills Index

READING/STUDY SKILLS

Comparing & contrasting ideas & information, 10, 11, 17-19, 22, 28, 30, 33, 38, 41, 45, 48-50, 52, 53, 55, 57-60

Constructing & interpreting pictures, tables, graphs, diagrams & symbols, 7-10, 13, 17, 20, 21, 23, 24, 26, 27, 29, 31, 32, 34, 35, 42-44, 46, 48, 49, 55, 56, 60

Distinguishing between scientific fact & opinion, 21, 22, 52

Following directions, 9, 12-16, 18, 19, 21, 23-25, 27, 28, 30, 32, 33, 39, 47, 52, 54, 56, 57, 59, 61, 62

Judging the relevance of information, 20, 39, 50, 51, 54, 61

Locating needed information in the library, 20, 23, 29, 37, 56, 58, 59

Reading for details, 24, 33, 50, 53, 62

Reading to find answers to questions, 7, 11, 13, 14, 16, 22, 26, 27, 31, 36, 37, 40-42, 44, 51

Summarizing, 43, 59

Taking notes, 24, 36, 40, 42, 44, 59

Writing scientific reports, 24, 26, 36, 37, 44

PROCESS SKILLS

Collecting, recording & analyzing data, 21, 22, 24, 27, 34, 36, 42, 44, 59, 61, 62

Describing, 9-18, 23-25, 27-31, 33, 36, 39, 40, 43, 44, 50, 53, 55, 57, 59

Drawing conclusions, 7-18, 20-34, 37-43, 47-62

Formulating models, 19, 22, 43, 59

Identifying problems & possible solutions, 18, 37-40, 47, 52

Measuring, 19, 23, 24, 28, 55

Observing, 7-10, 16, 17, 19-21, 23, 26-29, 32, 35, 40-42, 45, 46, 48, 49, 53-56, 58

Predicting, 7, 9, 11-15, 17, 22, 26, 28, 31-33, 37-44, 48, 51-54, 56, 58-61

Questioning, 7, 9-16, 18, 20, 21, 26-29, 31-33, 37, 38, 41, 48, 49, 52-56, 58-62

Sequencing, 9, 15, 17, 24, 42, 43

Sorting & grouping, 7, 9, 13-15, 23, 26, 27, 29, 52, 61

Using space/time relations, 23, 35

INTERPERSONAL RELATIONS AND ATTITUDES

Appreciating the beauty of nature, 8, 12, 13, 21, 23, 27, 29, 38

Appreciating ideas of others, 23, 50

Appreciating the history of science, 16, 20, 23, 24, 31, 32, 42, 49, 59

Communicating orally, in writing & in pictures, 9, 11-15, 17-19, 21, 22, 24, 26-30, 36-39, 43, 44, 52-54, 56, 57, 59

Cooperating, 9, 14, 15, 21, 23-25, 30, 32, 33, 50, 57

Demonstrating group work skills, 8, 9, 24, 30, 32, 45, 57

Developing an understanding of the relationships among science, technology and society, 7, 20, 33, 37, 46, 50

Developing a sense of responsibility, 18, 38-41, 47, 52

Developing decision making skills, 13, 39, 52, 62

Listening, 8, 9, 17, 29, 31, 32, 53, 54, 62

Relating scientific information to everyday experiences, 7, 10, 14-22, 26-28, 34, 36, 40, 42-45, 48, 50, 53-58, 60-62

Respecting rules and authority, 41, 52, 57

Understanding how our activities affect the environment, 37-44, 61